Prospect of Release

Prospect of Release

Tom Mandel

Chax Press   Tucson 1996

Front cover: *Outside*, 1989, steel sculpture
Back cover: *Inside*, 1989, steel sculpture

Manufactured in the USA by Cushing-Malloy, Inc., of Ann Arbor, Michigan.

ISBN 0-925904-11-2

Library of Congress Cataloging-in-Publication Data

Mandel, Tom
Prospect of release / Tom Mandel.
p. cm.
ISBN 0-925904-11-2 (alk. paper)
1. Sonnets, American. I. Title.
PS3563.A448P76 1996
811'.54--dc20 96-13879
CIP

for Paul Mandel

"The memory of the righteous is a blessing."

Speak Another Word

"Ich bin, auch hier, in Ihrer Gegenwart,
diesen Weg gegangen. Es war ein Kreis."

Paul Celan

That one is conscious and not know why
like cleaved rock or two that never joined
eyes blue in life become brown coals
silent as the Kodak into which they stare

from the rear of a backyard family gathering.
Brothers-in-law caper in the foreground.
Seasons, months, weeks, moments flatten

against the horizon, forgotten. To whom
now do I belong? An infinity of numbers
whose factor is three. I saw it was

a volume. At sea when I met him, light
poured in unrecalled, he offered no answers
to the questions I asked whose answers
were obvious, and I did not know why.

Of the ten things made at twilight
the greatest was '*speech-act*.' Think
of the orator moving in memory's rooms.
Imagination speaks, a matter of meaning,

internal volumes. It was like him to
know me. Articulate in perplexity, like
all bodies in a state of erratic motion

unless compelled to uniform motion or rest
by a mental law that unfolds phenomena
in time, words as it were want to live

their '*truth until the heavens*.' Thorough,
transparent, opaque, coded (undecoded),
tragedy studies us to divine our terms
of meaning. It is no absolute entity.

Clothes surround the body's points
to underscore its battle for insight.
As they are dressed they stand ready
in a time of distraction. We had not

prepared this story but gave ourselves
instructions. '*Place my body in a valley*
gather my bones into a cedar box

without your hands touching them. Put
a linen sheet over them, tear your
garments to the navel — all you are wearing

the suit that surrounds your frame.
Shovel dirt on me. Do for me what I did
for my father.' And I did for him
what he did for me. Do this for me.

As a full cup slides across thin ice
a wave somewhere stuns a shore
in the trembling world of names
a petal of wind blows his my way.

In profile, waiting to return, tell us
of daylight and darkness. Is it lonely
at the top? To the dying does a world

appear to begin again? During day lie in
an overturned bed, and right it at dusk.
The category of person straightens.

I followed your body to the grave,
as I will to my own. Where tragedy
studies us, fear its inheritance,
honor mother, father, the single name.

No paths lead among graves to articulate
our perplexity. Walking and thinking,
male, female, dust, frost and preservation.
No truth outside creation. Only truth within.

To praise you in bewilderment my soul
knows well, counting up ways as things
go wrong, as if the rest-stops along

a King's highway, without model of love
would lack commitment to meaning and fill
as traffic flows by, for how else should we

go on if not in these roles, enslaved to
meaning's delicate sense, identity and
difference our trespasses press upon us
as repetition transforms our route.

Who loosens, hands at their sides, a
force unfolding phenomena. What use is
resurrection when what we need is rain?
Like a full cup's surface, the document

trembles, a person in pitch darkness
dares to catch a glimpse of surroundings
during a lightning flash. Decision,

procedure. With every moment another law
descends the chute of words. Aware
of a continuing light, night for him

is like daytime, an overturned bed
turning within a few square feet,
from which he glimpses successive flashes
of rapid, always quickly fading light.

Study the esoteric text, don't turn
your face from it. There is no proper
articulation of what confronts '*the teaching*
of oneself,' leaving only '*a trace*

on the soul.' Encoded in desire
tragedy studies us. '*Some significances*
traced on the soul of a perfect

individual, if articulated linguistically
or expressed in metaphors would turn coarse
and elude one's design,' wrote Maimonides.

In the time taken to articulate a letter
we live and die in syntagmatic opposition
to God, the ultimate (escape of) meaning.
To deny anything is an act of perplexity.

Long I've lived with impetuous dynamism
moderate mystical alone a bachelor a titan
allusive among my books without regard
inseparable from an open conscious face

entertaining myself with vehicles friends
enemies neighbors the thought of borders
I had would wouldn't need again to cross.

Distinguished visitor foreign man mittel-
Europaischer Wundersohn inseparable
energetic one of a generation still to be.

Check my address in the garden so defined.
A full cup sliding across ice surrounds
my name in private path and public road.
A wave somewhere stuns a shore.

Invisible, at the switchboard, the effect
is like destiny, from which our eyes
slant out, enlarging to infinity, where
regressively space begins to picture

another child burst within a world we use.
Weeds in snow are pictures of desire.
Allusive, a titan entertained new values

to discover and establish as his life
explaining nothing I do save to make it
possible. The sky, itself predictable,

crowded with clouds. This writing cannot
be read; it is not duly registered. Do not
write my words, make no comment on them
streaked with black, alive with company.

To one who dies the world begins again
followed by words to describe it.
Youth and age, luminous with restraint
cleaved rock or two not joined. The dead

unite the clods of dirt that cover them
with instruction, their bones without
bare hands. I will do for him what

my father did for his. Landscape is
imperfect, moonlight to make it so.
In unwitting contribution the scientist

has taken to himself with love this
dead thing, vibrating the conscious use
of his own social maladjustment to
reveal a living act of revision.

In a private path a public road.
On the King's highway a mourner's band.
They follow him to his grave and will
to their own. Where the dead lie in right

the ground is whole, reverence modeled
on absence. '*Bury me beside my children.*'
What do you hear; what do you do?

For thirty days after death offer
consolation but do not ask the mourner
how he feels. Until twelve months

have passed, ask and offer. After
a year, no longer mention bereavement.
Don't lance his healed wound, or cure
her of a sickness that's past.

Who art kind and dealest kindly
Who art a true judge ruling over Thy work
We your people and servants in a place
where a miracle was wrought for us.

To give comfort wages war; to give thanks
for ourselves to one who is good.
A glass of water, daughters, this clay

figure, a cloud expanding in the still east,
tomorrow, the fruit that lays across
our laps, a phantom that passes our bed,

that love cover us, a cube, a ball, a piece
of tile, the referent calm to the touch
at arm's end, these are why we don't
punch the window out with our heads.

We malign those who disappear, their
realm is small, yet invoke their names
as our lives evoke theirs, words into
statement. Arms wrapped to the shoulder

in eternity, they cannot follow words.
Instead, our course changes to near
their grounds. Refracted in such frame,

prolific transcendent fatherly healed
cured constant, like indifference, does
affection prove illusion? No beaten

path nor Autobahn leads this way. A
letter, reflected in flame, senses
shoots to send. Unknowable, cemetery grass,
be wise — forget what we have known.

As you repeat the words of his lesson
the master appears to nod, but he is dying.
In his eyes a world seems to recommence.
His temples are destroyed, memory

fragmented with the lonely authority of
unspoken words. '*Your people dead, buildings*
down, city at my mercy, yet you resist'

turning within a few square pages,
compact, monotonous, unvoiced, victoryless,
a perfect snapshot of the formulated text.

Not stasis, neither gnosis is your goal.
To know more the reader must change,
feel so different, the exact transmission
of our rigorous oral tradition.

Momentum yearns to break the shape
of thought, to fly away through the square
of window behind his head, a social
maladjustment that would live in revision.

Open confidences made to train his eye
slit the bodily frame, its suitability
taken to himself, with love, skill of

human hand in a medium whose existence
is an absolute of justification, water
spilling from the fountain, all the village

dead. A range of tonal value lays beyond
the absolute where objects organize to express
causes whose effects they may yet become.
A valley, measured vision, linen sheets.

City I lived in and left capers in
pearls of its home town infernal alley.
A river should not run past your body
nor a path lead among the graves.

Remove the blue thread from your cloak,
the spittle from your soft palate.
Do not graze cattle on cemetery grass.

Don't go to stroll there, thinking *'here
is peace.'* Where the dead lie in right
the ground is whole, cannot be measured

nor divided for use. It is not a pasture
and I can give you nothing of it.
In a cemetery of exiles thought is
pestilence, to give comfort wages war.

Subtle, handsome vanity visits me.
Hands large, fingers long, face modeled
and content, a bare spark binding to
release, soul dances in the prospect.

Hands drew across his face. None to
comfort me but him, and he is gone.
My reverence is modeled on his absence

the absence of his lips and eyes. Dust
entered a window behind his head,
whirred in a shaft of Autumn light.

Winter light. Silent, a message it did
not bear but now suggests, long settled
like an issue, election or argument,
cleaved rock, or two that never joined.

Although he gave me his pasture
— *where this means the benefit of his*
advice, amusement and bemusement
at my values, love of them and of me —

he cannot give me his grave — *where*
this means access to his pain, to feel
for him, or his grave in place of mine,

release from our common fate, one
that binds me in my own torn clothes,
linen sheet — for my bones seal the same

earth as his, though I feel so different
— *do not graze cattle on cemetery grass,*
take no worldly benefit of it,
nor stroll in its peace to calm your spirit.

Who once turned naturally to accept
one's presence, a lowly authority
darkened the sky scattering stars
off the hammer blow, and nothing changed

but verbs; only nouns altered. Inconclusive
uncommon, sealed to life together
through the manifold rupture of attention's

bait of reference we belong to
each other as on the last day of childhood
following our visit to the grave.

Death frees no more than the dead
its '*No*' an act of perplexity for all,
a prospect of praise, long hands
drawn across lips in subtle vanity's act.

Do not comment on a fragment
of competence, nor write of my words
their luminous restraint, streaked
with black devices, mantling prey.

Like his word, the speaker's life will be
expounded independent of its linguistic
sense — orthography, gematria, calligraphic

flourishes to summon the canonical future.
Grief's code of desire cannot be read,
weeds in snow where progressively

space begins to be the sky itself,
predictable with clouds, a composition
design(at)ed for transmission. To discover
a set of values explains nothing I do.

All winds howl, but one does not
take up another to work the artifice
of our destiny out. In dreams we
see truth; dust they raise

with their feet reaches the Divine
Throne, a figure hunches in
a formula of sparks that speaks

a hammer's blow. Not stasis, not
gnosis your goal. Hold out for
the first thought, the best; think

and wait. The giver of the lesson
studies himself, teaching all day
until his own soul hangs from life
a thread hangs from his torn clothes.

The lonely say goodbye to be remembered.
Lawlike, not duly registered,
they are killed — only a phrase, '*the last day*
of childhood' — wiped out. A scribe

counts each letter that passes along
the king's highway and is not
what he was before another's words,

imagining looking into his eyes.
Minds have been trampled, seed and hull
destroyed. The story prepared for us

died, water spilling from the fountain
among the dead of a village.
Will there be new shoots again
in the field, the object's other side?

'You are powerless to disobey me,
for I know your name,' intones the macho
gnostic, rubbing his lamp until
the genie spits. A name is arbitrary,

void of essence, empty of presence,
not a being at all but a meaning.
When I named you, I knew your significance

but enjoyed no power over you. You were
good enough to respond. I called you
to respond to an insistent sound

of invitation. Will I be able to
address you still? Everything happens
in response to a thought. The events
of the world are only answers.

Like knees unabandoned mind must bend
and the category of person be the soul
clothed in time, the garment of a paradise
it has constructed. I prefer baked cake

to a handful of wheat, for nothing is known
without interpretation. Unarticulated,
a letter absorbs death, binds us end to

end, whereby the past avoids the present.
A day of rain, another day of dew alert us
to confusion, close our hands. Pages

blow past, petals on a wind, and bring
days singly, spoken things I learned
from him, bring meaning. Heeding
this word, a document springs to life.

To know, act on what you know.
A word in Greek exists thing-like;
all other languages mean nothing.
Speech the source and speech the flow.

What one knows changes, and I am sure
he died with the same love on his lips
that in his words was what he did

for me. It was nice to know him
who did not turn coarse nor elude design,
tipping out what filled him.

Contact in ambiguity. The value of
a sign is its isolation.
What questions of death remain,
coded in desire, we must ask ourselves.

Ten things were done at twilight,
one, two, four and five among them.
Hammer smashed rock, and sound stood forth.
Decision. He spoke, and it was.

'*Like dew, rain and snow descending*
to fructify earth, my word falls from my mouth
to do my will and does not return

unfulfilled but completes the task of my intentions.'
Walk out your door happily,
you will be led home secure.

Lonely at the top, where you wait
for a world seeming to start again.
Easy to tell of, as daylight is to tell
from darkness, tragedy studies us.

Lonely at the top? To say no is an act
of perplexity. Is not the value of a sign
its isolation? I thought to myself, '*God*
is nature,' but what did I mean?

A true judge ruling over his work bends
his creatures knees and causes them
to straighten, closes his creatures hands

and lets them loosen at their sides. He
takes the bread out of the earth — this loaf.
He creates the fruit of the earth — all

that's in the Safeway bin? Most of it
tastes like cardboard. Even moldy fruit?
I followed your body to its grave as if
the path led, and it does, to my own.

Sunlight falls on one decision, leaving
shadow for another, the ground of all
identity. A moment alters; stars chain
into form. A word brings on evening.

A letter opens her gates to the mind.
A vowel leaves preceding sounds alone.
Surrounding the body's points to clothe

its battle for insight, we had prepared
no story but were given instruction.
City I live in I leave; a river

does not run there. Seed and hull were
crushed, garment torn to the navel.
The ground I work is unmeasured,
whole. To give comfort wages war.

The author of the lonely — not to know more
nor to change, but to charm sparks off
a hammer blow, these and those the words
of the living God, stuck in empty space —

fell through the mirror and was broken.
Its cracks reflect his other side — one
word, many meanings. Gnosis is no goal.

Dust, frost and preservation my address to
the garden so defined. Probably unable
to breathe, his face darkens; spittle dries;

blue pulls out of his eyes, and he dies.
His sky chars inward to vision's edge.
A cardinal settles on its branch like a rock.
The force of instruction rips his clothes.

Like the living the dead are many,
connected in all traces to the common
social order. Broken, these connections
signal death, and in turn we allow

the soul release from its body. Opening
an envelope does not free us from its
message, who shoulder manifold traces

to live on, bound to each other
in new ways, as we were and now are,
living bound to the dead and each other.

The knife comes out clean; the cake
is done. Why does time pass? Because one
observes a rule. Why wear clothes? To model
a soul in paradise, clothed in its days.

Out of focus, attentionless, repressed, a
perfect snapshot of the clothes we were wearing,
'*Messiah*' (history) inverts language,
the look in its eye remembered.

In the most minimal space, four cubits,
a student sits with a formulated text, law
stacked in empty space, to memorize it.

He gave me instruction without touching
my hands, comfort without seeing me.
Although we spoke without understanding

each other, I understood him when we spoke
as he did me. Do this for me. We lie in
an overturned bed. In a private path
a public road, buried beside the children.

Darken the sky — char mirror to rim. Hedge
round me with a low fence, I'd be seen
not known, the sky where once I burned.
Buried on his back under rubble and trees

a cardinal sang to branch-borne weight
of abandoned genus, buried as storm broke.
Force of instruction to rip these clothes

like a rock that sleeps all day, mantled
in its wings, imperfect bait of reference
calm abandon muses on his name, high

as principle, long as a day is honest,
a bare spark binds to release. I drank
from your source as drinks from darkness.
I danced at the prospect of release.

Wish to die ourselves? Immense rush of
tomorrow from its East. Abandon what
you fear abandons you, nature, character
brushed back with calm at the end of

harm, an act of charity, charm, refrain
metamorphosed whose good guttural people
now united buried under grass our dead

and the words from which these I write
have grown anew. Walking and thinking,
male and female, the wild German garden,

awning, guardrail, heart's rein defined.
Dust, frost and preservation. Swing
finger to cheek to check for growth,
its art refined in words you've sown.

Shoots are trampled, seed and hull crushed.
Cracks in a mirror reflect the object's other
side, dust that rises when we write,
a successive synthesis of consonants in mind.

Wind howls, yet its vowels let lie
preceding sounds, a hierarchy of artifice
to work out as destiny. The palate dries

within sounds. Consonants clothe the soul.
Difference, discernment. The senses are
social product, a suit ripped to the navel.

Sealed in a single pipeline of attention
no conclusions change thought's shape,
shatter this, concentrated to a point
of certain death, certainty of death.

One spoke, and the document's pages riffled.
Things stood up, interpretation began.
An infinity of numbers whose factor is three
sprang into non-spatial being (meaning).

The wind trembled like a full cup
sliding through time. With every letter
of a name, the named mood altered.

Soon one could tell daylight from darkness,
discernment from difference. In every cloak
we threw over our shoulders, a blue thread

signaled life. Creatures began to write works
that could not be read, they were not
duly registered. The oval of a long-dead
face appeared but did not comfort me.

I am he who said to the world '*Stop!*'
for if I had not said '*Stop!*' to
the heavens and '*Stop!*' to the earth
they would have expanded until this

very moment. I speak to establish my
isolation from you, the object of
my address, whose silence unattainable

listens but cannot respond. Only tears
interrupt such words; tears are
a trope for the presence of the dead.

Interrupting each other thus, we make
language whole, grounding in speech
both isolation and resolution. We give
exemplary articulation to life and death.

Its significance escapes, face to face,
into the force of instruction, charm
trapped in eternity, on the shoulder,
inarticulate, leaving no shadow

for meaning. Do not turn away from
the teaching of oneself to value a sign
in isolation, guardrail, bare spark,

a cardinal flash on a dead branch
of science leaves its trace on the soul
whose source and flow are speech.

A titan allusive, an ultimate letter
chants the text it changes, and in
contact is ambiguity, one word from
many meanings buried under grass.

An infinity of numbers whose factor is three.
But, one, two and four are not among them.
They raised dust with their feet, until
it reached the Divine Throne. Lips and

mouth express the sense of writing
contained in words, contained in letters,
marks of script a mind seizes to synthesize.

Do you prefer baked cake or a heap of wheat?
In the artifice of dream one sees truth,
a wave of words somewhere, severed from land,

seven years lean and seven plenty.
These and those, sealed to conclusion.
The wound is gone, not even a scab. Don't
heal it, nor minister to sickness past.

Because power sought out authority
to kill it, the givers of tradition perished.
We hear words in fragmented memories
of the lowly, who have no authority

of their own. When you say goodbye
(to die), speak the law and be remembered.
Hold back, hold out for the first word

whenever it shall come. For the best thought,
the first thought, think and wait. My father
died on the last day of my childhood.

When the temple was destroyed, God lost
all in this world, and left four cubits
of law. The giver of lessons dies as we
repeat a figure, hunched in its formulas.

Inverse to language, order speculates
in res: words, new shoots in a field
where mind was trampled. Feel so
different (saying them), felt so

free, looking in your eyes. To one
whose world begins again, everything
signifies this fact whose own significance

is infinite. Halted seemingly forever,
inscribed but not written, spittle
dried at the back of your mouth,

blue threads pulled from your fringes,
tremble. Do this for me; honor inheritance.
Don't stroll, however brightly stars
there shine, in cemetery darkness.

Difficult to think beyond the letter
in advance of creation, combined
in an infinite story, not what we were
before a scribe counted every letter.

Creation could have been other, and is,
than it is. A world of letters? Cartoon
note-forms pouring from a horn-flourish?

When you speak another's words, imagine
him saying them while looking into
your eyes. When you speak your own words

to another, look him in the eye; accept
the meaning of your words. The old seat
of power doesn't return. Underline
his insights, the strength of transmission.

What questions are left concerning, or at
the moment of, death? The source is speech
and its flow is speech. One, two,
four and five are not among them. Truth

proceeds from the education of the mind,
a voice heard without articulated words.
They sat on both sides of me, took my hands

as I lay crying in the bed I then rose
to straighten. Dusk fell, the sky
at the rim of the hills red as a petal.

Like a full cup sliding across thin ice
I tipped out what had filled me, a sequence
of consonants in calligraphic flourish
heard all at once, then gone at once.

Nature, caprice of culture, invention of man.
We cannot read this writing but we speak.
Must time meet each with what he needs?
No figure on the final day hunched in

choral formula, but all his words have
many meanings. To learn more turn to
the esoteric text. Let chant equal change

for the knower must change. To whom now
do I belong? This loaf of rye, this peach,
what do they mean? An idol is perplexing

thought; a false proposition turns present
to memory, caught on the infinitesimal
difference between his body and my soul.
Between a term and what it means.

A significant line leads to certain death,
one of rhythmic emotional intensity
that fears all concentration vibrating
backwards into a third dimension.

What he took to himself with love, he
left with the same love on his lips.
Our lives explain nothing we do except

to make it possible. Do not speak of these
words, but repeat them, accompany me,
understand the strength of transmission,

the authority of the lonely in the meaning
of words, new shoots in the field.
Power killed the transmitter of tradition.
The old seat of power won't return.

Not all who speak understand what
they say — history, like nature, an idol
formed from false propositions. Rainy
day above the day of resurrection.

These and these. Its attributes are his
and ours. In a bewilderment all know
question praises answer. To say no

is an act of perplexity before unfolding
phenomena in time, the procedure of
creation. We cannot express the measure

we've apprehended thoroughly, orderly
as in other sciences. Yet emanation and
concealment do not equal faintness.
Why do people continue in darkness?

He lifts and falls, the feather on a wing,
dancing at the prospect of release. Handsome,
vain, he is bound to us still in subtle ways
by new shoots of law in the field.

The story that prepared us died. The last guest
gone, the couch you taught from overturned.
Not duly registered but prepared to say

the same thing, to mean something
different, a rigorous oral tradition waits
for us; the author of its lonely book

cannot be read, and others the category
of person has not written. Cleaved
rock, it was nice to know you.
Broken tablets, to pasture in your tabernacle.

I and you alone are two. Four and five
outside the infinity whose factor
is three. I address you, bare spark
but not alive; does another listen?

I heard an awesome voice without articu-
lation of words, since when I've begun
to stutter, but what do I mean?

Lonely at the top? Not all who speak
understand what they say. Like knees
mind must bend. Do not abandon the world

to nature, for there is none, only
idols formed of false propositions.
Decision. Vowels, bring on morning.
Consonants, cause the sun to set.

At once each thought calls for and contains
an answer. Chosen, called, addressed.
The ground of this answer is whole.
A speech-act made at twilight teaches

us day and night. I can give you
nothing, except to make it possible.
The King's highway leads *past*, not

to nor *from*, bearing meaning away,
a summons. I may do my will on what
I have made of nothing; when I call,

it stands up to do my will, becoming
what it is. He calls, and the answer is
to be what's named, the category
of person, '*truth til the heavens*.'

Often I ask a question whose answer is
known, question praising answer in advance.
To whom now do I belong? Distant,
flattened against the horizon of a past

more or less forgotten, recalled only
by these words describing it, no more
than nouns alter, verbs change only.

If we deserved defeat we would await it.
We merit accident instead. '*Stop!*' he said
'*O world, if you must, it's been nice*

knowing you.' Their departures separated
by decades of life, they return a pair,
unconscious of each other but aware of me,
present to my grief, distant and comforting.

You are my second, one says to the other,
whom repetition changes and explains,
bearer of identity, yet other —
my stand-in and myself. I must distract

you while you wait to return. Lonely at
the top? Truly they follow to their own
the body they trail to its grave. Daylight

lies in an overturned bed. Moonlight
glistens along imperfect lengths of beam.
One whom I thought abandoned me returned.

Another I asked to stay must leave.
From you I learn better and now know why
each mind must bend, but only to its task,
soul dancing at the prospect of release.

About the Author

Tom Mandel was born in Chicago in 1942, the American child of Austrian Jews fleeing Hitler. He was educated in Chicago's public schools and jazz/blues clubs, and at the University of Chicago. He has lived in New York, Paris and San Francisco, and now resides in Washington DC.

Tom Mandel is the author of ten books of poetry. His first book, *Ency* (Tuumba, 1978), was a foundational work in the early history of Language Poetry. Recent books include *Four Strange Books* (GAZ, 1990), *Realism* (Burning Deck, 1991) and *Letters of the Law* (Sun & Moon, 1994). In 1996, Zasterle Press (Islas Canarias, España) will publish Tom Mandel's chapbook *Ancestral Cave*, and Potes & Poets will issue *Absence Sensorium*, a book length poem written by Tom Mandel in collaboration with the poet Daniel Davidson.

In addition to his life as a poet, which takes place during the twenty four hours each day comprises, Tom Mandel is an entrepreneur, president of a software company in the information systems / Internet industry.

Chax Press

Founded in 1984 in Tucson, Arizona, Chax Press returned to Tucson in the summer of 1996 after a 3-year residence in Minneapolis. The press publishes books in editions which explore the possibilities of the art of the book, and in literary trade paperback editions.

The typefaces used in *Prospect of Release* are Goudy and Gill Sans. The book has been designed by Charles Alexander.

Other Chax Press Books

Myung Mi Kim, *The Bounty*
Mary Margaret Sloan, *The Said Lands, Islands, and Premises*
Norman Fischer, *Precisely the Point Being Made*
Nathaniel Tarn, *Caja del Rio*
Rosmarie Waldrop, *Fan Poem for Deshika*
Lisa Cooper, *The Ballad in Memory*
Nathaniel Mackey, *Outlantish*
Ron Silliman, *Demo to Ink*
Beverly Dahlen, *A Reading 8-10*
Gil Ott, *Wheel*
Karen Mac Cormack, *Quirks & Quillets*

Susan Bee & Charles Bernstein, *Fool's Gold*
Sheila Murphy, *Teth*
bp Nichol, *Art Facts: A Book of Contexts*
Charles Bernstein, *Four Poems*
Larry Evers & Felipe S. Molina, *Wo'i Bwikam/Coyote Songs*
Mei-mei Berssenbrugge, *Mizu*
Charles Alexander, *Hopeful Buildings*
Lyn Hejinian & Kit Robinson, *Individuals*
Eli Goldblatt, *Sessions*
John Randolph Hall, *Zootaxy*
Paul Metcalf, *Firebird*
Karl Young, *Five Kwaidan in Sleeve Pages*
Charles Alexander, *Two Songs*
Paul Metcalf, *Golden Delicious*
Jackson Mac Low, *French Sonnets*

Forthcoming in 1996/1997 from Chax Press

Karen Mac Cormack, *The Tongue Moves Talk*
Lisa Cooper, *& Calling It Home*
Hank Lazer, *Three of Ten*